LARRY
THE FARTING
LEPRECHAUN

JANE BEXLEY

ISBN 9798701849219

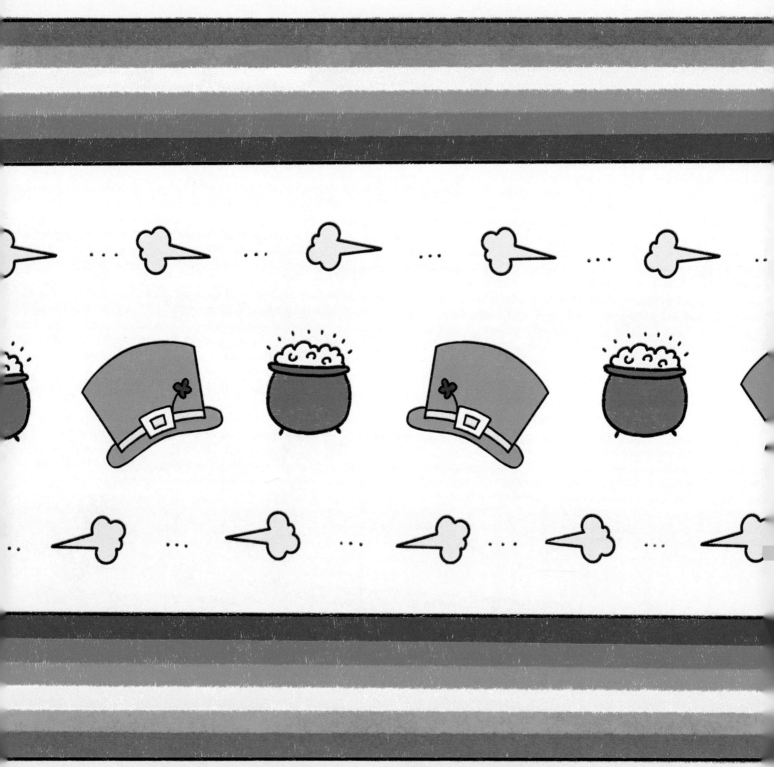

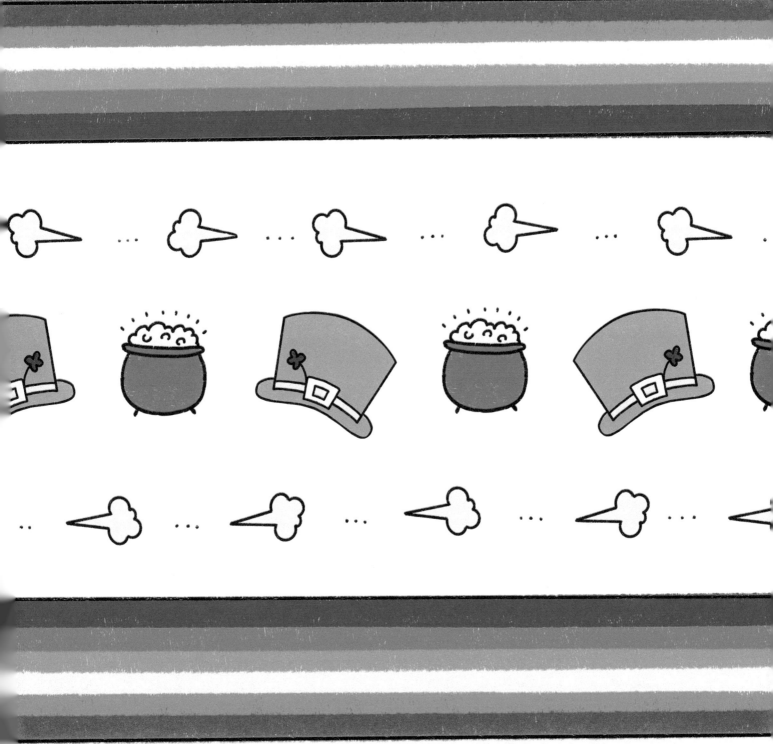

Larry the Leprechaun loves making mischief. He loves playing silly tricks and making funny messes in classrooms and houses. Leprechauns need to be sneaky, fast, and quiet to get away without getting caught.

Larry is very sneaky...

and very fast...

...but being quiet is a BIG problem. Larry has a lot of gas and noisy toots. Usually Larry thinks toots are pretty funny, but they are definitely NOT funny when he needs to be quiet. His noisy bum has gotten him into some sticky (and stinky) situations!

FART!

TOOT!

THUNDER BUNS

A round of Thunder Buns is the worst when Larry is trying to hide. This is when toot bombs explode with a thunderous BOOM! Cracking loud farts is not a good way to be sneaky or stay hidden.

LAUGHING GAS

Laughing Gas is another one of Larry's biggest problems. Sometimes when Larry plays a funny trick he laughs so hard that he farts. The roar of his laugh and fart combined is loud enough to give away his hiding spot!

FART ATTACK

Leprechaun traps are extra dangerous for Larry. Even if he doesn't get caught in the trap, he could get really scared and have a Fart Attack where he rips a ton of noisy toots all at once. A big noise like that could really get him in trouble.

SQUAT SQUEAKERS

Larry's gas also causes problems when he isn't trying to be sneaky, like when he's exercising. Larry usually lets a few Squat Squeakers fly at the gym. The other leprechauns do not find it very funny.

ONE CHEEK SNEAK

Larry has tried everything he can think of to keep his booty quiet. Sometimes he tries the One Cheek Sneak and lets his gas go in tiny, quiet puffs instead of one big blast.

PANTS PINCHER

Sometimes he tries a Pants Pincher to hold it back until he's in a safe place to let it go.

KNICKER RIPPER

Sometimes the Pants Pincher doesn't work and it turns into a Knicker Ripper.

FART AND DART

Most of the time Larry's gas explodes without warning so his only choice is to Fart and Dart. He lets it rip and takes off running!

PIPE POPPERS

Even though Larry's toots get him into a bit of trouble when he needs to be quiet, his farts can be pretty fun the rest of the time. Larry loves blowing Pipe Poppers. Double the bubbles!

LUCKY LOOT TOOT

Larry's favorite fart is the Lucky Loot Toot. When leprechauns find a pot of gold they get so excited that they fart! Larry loves these special little gas fluffs because he gets to fart with his friends, which is the BEST way to fart.

CROP DUSTING

Larry enjoys Crop Dusting the clover fields to let his farts fly free. He also thinks it helps the shamrocks grow a little greener, but he can't be 100% sure.

STINKY STEPPERS

Like all Leprechauns, Larry loves to dance. But all the jumping around shakes up Larry's tummy, and you know what that means!

Thankfully the music is always loud enough to hide the sound of his Stinky Steppers, or tiny dance toots, that escape with every Irish step.

RAINBOW ROCKET

Sometimes leprechaun toots are both fun and useful. When Larry needs to get somewhere really fast, he blasts a power-packed Rainbow Rocket and takes off into the sky.

The next time you see a rainbow, a bright green shamrock, or a mysterious mess, take a second to listen very closely. If you hear the magical sound of tiny toots, there's a good chance you've just had a visit from Larry the Leprechaun!

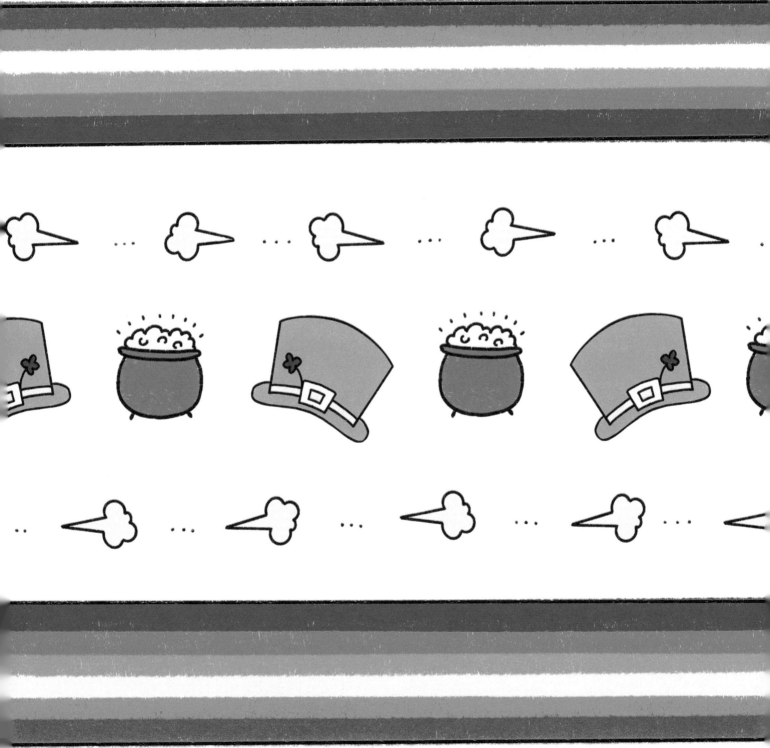